Grandpa and t...

1

Nelson

Trog and Father were looking for nuts
and berries to eat.
They were deep in the forest
where they had never been before.

Suddenly, a loud trumpeting noise
came from behind some tall trees.

'What's that?' whispered Trog.

'I don't know what it is,' said Father,
'but I am going to have a look.'

'I'm frightened,' said Trog.

'So am I,' said Father,
'but let's have one peep at it.'

4

They walked on very slowly
and then they saw it.
It was a mammoth,
the biggest animal they had ever seen.

'My goodness,' said Father,
'do you see what I see?'

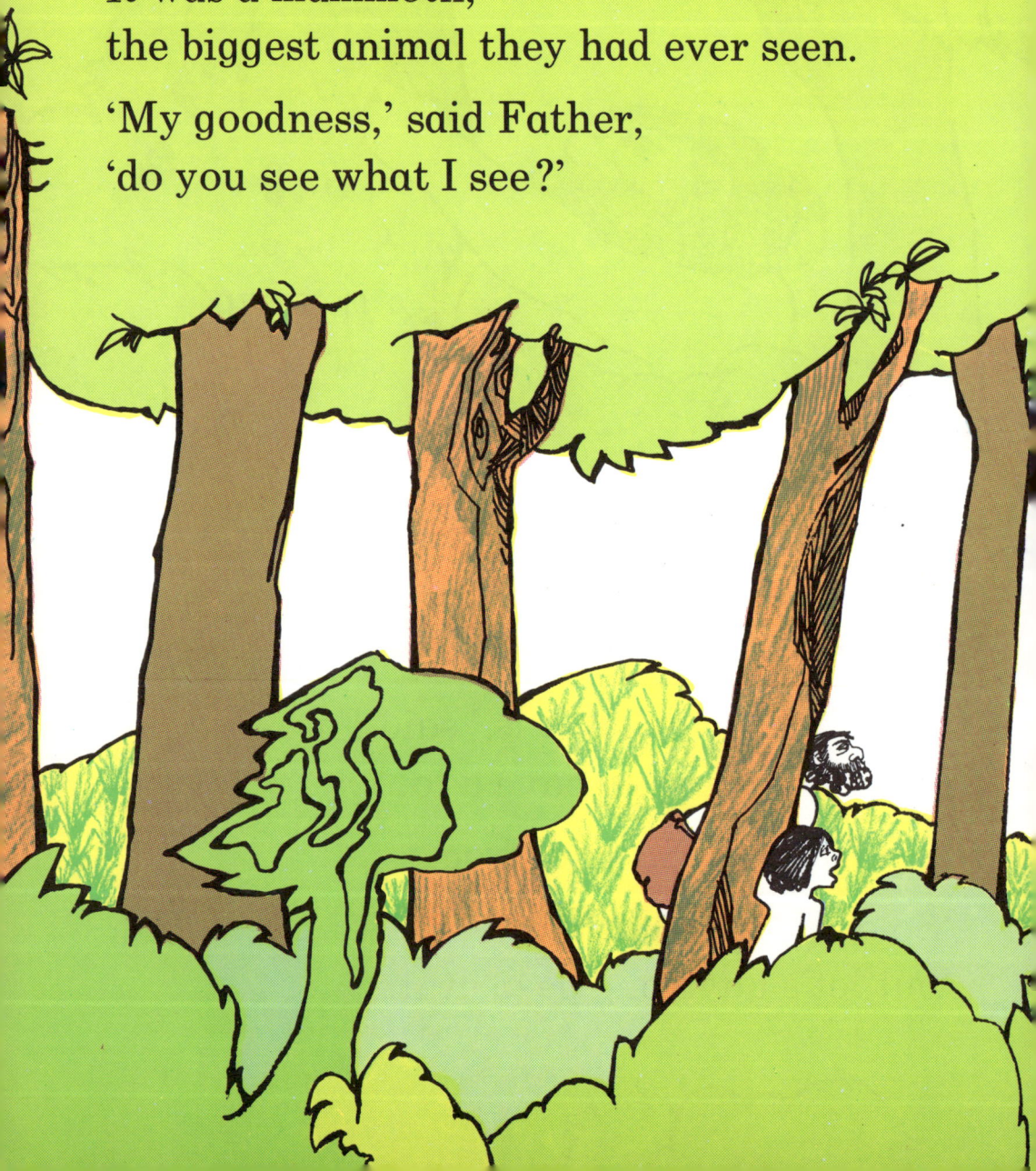

'I jolly well do,' said Trog,
'and I'm off.'

'I am too,' said Father.
'We must crawl back slowly
or he will see us,
and I should not like to make him angry.
I have never seen anything like him
in all my life.'

Slowly,
the two of them began to crawl backwards,
watching the mammoth all the time.

Trog did not see a deep hole behind him
and he fell into it with a crash.

'Help!' Trog shouted.

'Sh!' whispered Father.

'Help!' Trog shouted again.

'Keep quiet and lie still,'
whispered Father,
'or he will see us.'

sh! sh!

Father and Trog lay very still
but the great animal came towards them.

'If we move he will get us,' said Father.

The mammoth came up to the hole
and looked down at Trog.
Trog lay very still.
It put its long trunk down into the hole,
lifted Trog up like a feather,
and gave him to Father.
They both stood looking up at the mammoth
and the mammoth looked down at them.

'What do we do now?' asked Trog.

'Let's run,' said Father.

They ran out of the forest
as fast as they could
but the mammoth crashed after them.
Then they walked,
but so did the mammoth.

'I think he's going to follow us
all the way home,' said Father.

'Wait until Grandpa sees him,' said Trog,
'he'll have a fit.'

They walked the rest of the way home and when the mammoth saw the huts he stopped.

Trog and Father ran to find Mother and Grandpa.

Trog ran into Grandpa's hut.

'Come and see
what we found in the forest,' he said.
'I don't know what it is
but it's as big as ten horses.'

'Ten horses?' said Grandpa.
'Don't be silly.'

It has two tails,' said Father.

'Two tails?' cried Grandpa.

'Yes,' said Trog,
'one big tail at the front
and a little one at the back.
It picked me up with the front one.'

'And it has two horns,' said Father.

'Two horns?' said Grandpa.
I must see this thing.'

'There it is,' said Trog.
He pointed to the mammoth by the trees.

Grandpa took one look
and ran back into his hut.

'Come out, Grandpa,' said Trog.
'He won't hurt you.'

'That's what you say,' said Grandpa.
'He could squash me flat with one foot.'

'Well, **I'm** not frightened,' said Trog.
'I shall call him Tiny for fun.'

'If you are not frightened,
then I'm not,' said Grandpa,
and he came out of his hut.

The mammoth put out his long trunk
but Grandpa knocked it away.

In a flash
Tiny picked up Grandpa in his trunk,
and ran round the huts.

'Stop him!' yelled Grandpa.
'Stop him!'

'We can't,' shouted back Trog.
'He's too big. Nothing can stop him!'

stop
him

'Do something!' yelled Grandpa again.

'Pull on his ears!' shouted Father.

Grandpa pulled one of Tiny's big ears and the mammoth stopped running. Grandpa slid to the ground.

Again Tiny put out his trunk
but this time Grandpa patted it
and all was well.

'I don't want any more rides with him,'
Grandpa said.
'He is so big.
But what use is he? What can he do?'

'We don't know,' Father said.
'He must be able to do something.
Think how strong he is.'

The next day it was very cold.

'It will soon be winter,' said Mother.
'It is time
for you all to go to the forest
and bring back some wood.'

'I do hate that job,' said Grandpa.
'It's such hard work chopping trees down
and dragging them home.'

'I know,' said Mother,
'but we must have wood
to put on the fire in the winter.'

'What about Tiny?' asked Grandpa.
'He may follow us and get in the way.
I don't want him near me.'

'Well,' said Father,
'we will go first and Tiny will follow us.
You can go later
to a different part of the forest.'

'That's a good idea,' said Grandpa.

Trog and Father took their flint axes
and set off, but Tiny did not move.

Grandpa waited and waited
and then he crept away.
'Good,' he said to himself.
'He's not following me.'

In the forest, Grandpa found a small tree
and set to work.
After a few swings with his axe
he looked round
and there was Tiny watching him.

'What a big useless thing you are!'
said Grandpa.

Then Tiny walked up to the tree
and put his great head against it.
He gave a little nod of his head
and the tree went crashing to the ground.

'My goodness!' said Grandpa.
'That was quick!'

He struggled and struggled
to pick up the tree
but it was too much for him.

Grandpa looked at Tiny.
Tiny looked at Grandpa
and then at the tree.
Quickly the great animal
lifted it up.

'Come on, Tiny,' said Grandpa.
'Let's show Trog the work I have done.'

He walked back home.
Tiny came behind him,
carrying the tree.

When they reached home,
Tiny put down the tree
and went off to the river to drink.
Grandpa found Mother cooking the dinner.

'You are soon back,' she said to him.
'Was the work too much for you?'

'Don't be silly,' said Grandpa.
'Look at that tree.
You don't know how strong I am.'

Mother looked at the tree
that Tiny had brought back.

'You are stronger than I thought,'
she said to him.

'I don't know what you would all do
without me,' said Grandpa.

When it was nearly dark,
Trog and Father came back
carrying a small tree between them.

'Where have you two been all day?'
asked Grandpa.

'Where have we been all day?' said Trog.
'It's hard work chopping a tree down.
Where is your wood for the winter?'

'It's over there,' said Grandpa.
'It didn't take me long.'

'I don't understand how he did it,'
said Trog to Father.
'That's a big tree for one man
to fetch from the forest.'

'He's much stronger than I thought,'
Father said.
'Much stronger.'

Every day Tiny followed Grandpa
to the forest.

He pushed bigger and bigger trees down.

Trog and Father were never back
until very late.

'How on earth do you do it?'
they asked Grandpa.

'It's easy,' said Grandpa.
'It's easy when you are as strong as I am.'

But one morning,
Father and Trog waited
until Grandpa had gone to the woods
with Tiny.

They followed him and hid.

They saw Grandpa
take one swing with his axe at a tree
and then sit down
while Tiny pushed the tree over
and picked it up.

Trog and Father came out.

'So that's how you do it,'
they said to him.
'Well, from now on
we will take Tiny with us.
You can go on your own.
Let's see you chop down as big a tree
as you say you can.
That will teach you to tell us
how strong you are!'

'Oh dear,' said Grandpa.
'That's done it!'